What Our Readers Have Said...

"The Pinpoint Training Series delivers information that could be used in a lot different areas."

•

"Applicable and valid. The information is good."

•

"I like this because I can take them with me to read at a convenient time. I feel the little time I have to spend in the office is best use on activities that directly relate to revenue opportunities. I like the short amount of time it takes to keep up with these."

•

"I like the fact that the format allows the books to be reviewed as time permits. All work has been conducted on personal, evening/weekend time."

•

"My thought is that the real value of these books comes into effect when doing the action plans."

•

"The challenge when I think a specific topic does not apply is to find a way to make it apply."

•

"Short and sweet. These books are easy to comprehend."

•

"These books are very easy to read and clearly outlined."

•

"I have enjoyed reading these books. They are relevant to today's work environment and the ongoing change in the way we manage our workforce."

•

"I believe the contents of the Pinpoint series are excellent. It causes one to reflect on the daily dynamics in working with oneself as well as with management and peers."

•

"Most of the information in these would help an open-minded management person, or an inexperienced management person."

•

"These books will pay for the time that I am investing. There are numerous good ideas that will streamline what I do and how I do it."

•

"All and all I think the Pinpoint series is a good program. I know other people I would love to have something like this. I think a lot of the suggestions are very useful, and can be applicable to everyday situations. If nothing else it's a good reference guide to fall back upon if a situation arises in the future."

•

"These books reinforce many concepts that I have learned through seminars, schooling and other programs. For myself, it serves as a constant learning tool that keeps me on top of the issues that many of us encounter every day."

•

"All in all, I think you have good training books. It helps everyone to review these materials, it serves as a good reminder to us on how to conduct ourselves."

•

"The information is valuable in these books."

•

Time & Personal Management

Pinpoint Sales Management Skill Development Training Series

TIMOTHY F. BEDNARZ

MAJORIUM
BUSINESS PRESS

Pinpoint Sales Management Skill Development Training Series
"Time & Personal Management"
Timothy F. Bednarz

Graphic design: Monika Pawlak

Majorium Business Press
2025 Main Street
Stevens Point, WI 54481
715.342.1018 • 800.654.4935

ISBN 978-1-882181-46-9

Printed in the United States of America

Introduction

The Pinpoint Sales Management Skill Development Training Series is designed for targeted training and education regarding increased improvement in a specific skill or competency.

Each book within this series is designed to be easy to use, understand and apply to your job. It can be used as a basis for training individuals, as a discussion guide or as a personal training tool.

Each chapter within this book discusses a specific concept. When you have completed all eight chapters you should have a 360º perspective of the topic.

Additionally, each chapter is divided into specific sections:

- The first section provides you with an overview of the topic
- The Implications section discusses why the concept is important, and why it is important to learn and apply.
- The Strategies, Tips & Techniques to Apply section teaches how to use and apply the particular concept to your work.
- The Points to Ponder section gives you something to think about or to be discussed with a group setting. These are questions not meant to be immediately answered, but to be pondered over time.
- The Training Activity section provides you with the tools to transfer what you have learned to your job. It is designed to help create an action plan to effectively apply the concept.

Each of the topics in this series is time-tested and proven in the marketplace. They have been used by thousands of employees as training tools. Many of the users have commented that what made these books valuable, was the ability to refer to them when a problem surfaced. They indicated that they remembered reading about the exact problem. They referred back to these books and found an appropriate solution.

You will find them equally valuable as a resource in your professional development library.

Table of Contents

LEARNING OBJECTIVES:

- To establish effective goals and objectives.
- To set priorities.
- To delegate tasks.
- To deal with interruptions and time wasters.
- To become more effective managers.

1

Organizational Statements

Neither salespeople nor sales managers regulate, govern and guide their activities in a void. Time management and personal goal setting must be closely linked to the specific goals and objectives established by senior management. These are generally communicated through a series of organizational statements that are designed to identify and direct key activities that must be achieved and sustained in order for companies to maintain and enhance their market presence, viability and growth potential.

IMPLICATIONS — WHAT THIS MEANS TO YOU

Sales managers often find themselves in a precarious position between senior sales managers, who direct and oversee their companies' key activities while continually demanding increased performance, and their sales forces that must be continually motivated to generate revenue.

Before sales managers can competently manage their own time and activities, it is important to understand how they fit into the organizational structure and impact the overall performance of their company. This can be done by analyzing how certain organizational statements are meant to guide their activities and how they can be used to define existing needs to successfully bridge gaps between expected company-related courses of direction, objectives and goals, and those of individual sales forces and other salespeople.

Many sales managers succumb to the pitfall of separating their company's targets and objectives from their salesperson's defined and established goals. They also tend to ignore certain objectives when directing their own personal activities and performance.

It is important for sales managers to understand that they are liaisons between their company and the salespeople they lead. It is their role and responsibility to assure that all activities contribute to the achievement of specific company-related goals and objectives. Faced with daunting pressures, many sales managers attempt to fit their regional performance goals into company objectives after the fact, rather than using corporate goals and objectives to guide their ongoing activities throughout the year.

STRATEGIES, TIPS & TECHNIQUES TO APPLY

Organizational statements are strategic in nature. They are generally created by senior management officials and are specifically designed to communicate overall company values. This ensures consistency of thought and action throughout individual organizations. Secondly, they are designed to control and direct key activities throughout individual companies. This is to guarantee that all activities essential to corporate success are fully identified, defined and organized to meet established goals and objectives. These become the building blocks and guideposts for selected activities that should be incorporated and implemented.

In order to fully comprehend how to successfully manage time and responsibilities, it is essential to analyze how the hierarchy of organizational statements directly impacts sales managers' professional duties.

The Vision Statement

The concept of "vision statement" is fairly new to corporate business. It is commonly found in entrepreneurial companies, although many larger organizations are beginning to incorporate vision statements into their overall strategic planning.

Vision statements are the broadest of strategic planning concepts. They are a means of incorporating initial founders' or entrepreneurs' dreams into formalized guiding statements for their particular organizations. Vision statements outline and define the overall direction and chartered course that individual companies wish to take. On the micro level, sales managers can develop vision statements to create an overall direction for their own personal lives and careers.

Mission Statements

Mission statements are developed by senior management and normally are not altered or changed. They can be reviewed and updated as circumstances change, or when the need exists for individual companies to evolve and transform themselves. However, modifications occur rather infrequently.

Mission statements are used to comprehensively define individual organizations. They identify what particular companies intend to provide and the markets and individuals they expect to serve. They are meant to provide salespeople with an overall course of action to pursue and, as such, contribute guidance and direction.

Corporate Goals and Objectives

Goals are strategic in nature and are meant to provide long-term direction. Objectives are tactical and provide short-term direction. Companies generally have set corporate goals for three- to five-year time spans. However, with the onset of technology, most corporate goals need to be set for 18- to 36-month periods. Any planning beyond 36 months tends to get ambiguous and oftentimes inaccurate or outdated.

Corporate goals and objectives are meant to provide immediate direction for all organizational departments and salespeople. Salespeople's goals and objectives as well as those of support staff need to be directly related to and intertwined with specifically defined corporate goals and objectives.

Departmental Goals and Objectives

Departmental goals and objectives are defined through corporate goals and objectives. Typically, vice presidents use specifically defined goals and objectives to direct and oversee their various departments. Within departments, these goals become the basis for defining and directing all key activities. Vice presidents generally develop specific goals for all functions within specific departmental levels. Additionally, goals and objectives generally are defined and established for regional sales managers and supervisors.

Regional Goals and Objectives

Regional goals and objectives generally are defined and established by vice presidents, which are then assigned to individual regional sales managers. They in turn develop their own goals based upon the expected regional objectives and targets. As they proceed to implement specific individual goals, quotas and objectives for salespeople within particular geographic regions, it becomes essential to focus their planning efforts on structuring and detailing activities best suited to achieving the regional objectives.

Goals and Objectives

Once salespeople are assigned specific goals and objectives, they can begin to plan their year's selling activities around meeting or exceeding them. In this manner, they can subsequently begin to develop time management plans as well as detail specific strategies for enhancing and maximizing their personal performance.

POINTS TO PONDER – SOMETHING TO THINK ABOUT

1. How closely do you pay attention to the goals and objectives presented to you by your superiors and senior management?
2. Do you actively use corporate goals and objectives to guide and direct your department's activities for the year?

TRAINING ACTIVITY — APPLICATION & ACTION PLAN

1. Review and familiarize yourself with your company's mission statement, as well as all of its corporate and departmental goals.
2. Identify the flow of goals from senior management to your own particular area of responsibility.
3. Determine if your departmental goals and objectives are fully aligned with those of upper management and the organization.
4. Identify what needs to be done to correct any misalignment of your departmental goals with those of the company.
5. Determine specific steps that need to be taken in order to maximize your workforce's performance.

2

Setting and Attaining Goals

Many sales managers have attained their positions as a result of being successful and effective salespeople. However, the skills required to achieve success as a frontline salesperson are quite different from those required for successful managing.

One of the most important skills that sales managers need to master relates to the organization of their time and resources. To do this effectively, they must know how to set and achieve specific goals and objectives. They cannot successfully manage their salespeople unless they are able to adequately manage themselves.

IMPLICATIONS – WHAT THIS MEANS TO YOU

Sales managers are under intense pressure to produce results. Ongoing success requires effective goal setting skills for both themselves and those they manage.

While goal setting on the surface appears a simple process, it takes both experience and expertise to know how to develop specific objectives and outcomes that consistently move sales managers, salespeople and companies forward.

If goals are too daunting, sales managers and their people will be overwhelmed, dispirited and frustrated. This accomplishes nothing. If goals are set too low, they will be easily overlooked. The art of goal setting is to create a balance. Goals should be set to the point where they stretch the abilities of everyone involved in order to achieve them.

IBM built a highly successful sales strategy upon the principle that "Success builds success." Sales managers set small but attainable goals for their salespeople that were successfully accomplished in smaller and effective increments. They found that immediate successes made the next expected steps easier to attain.

This is important for sales managers to consider because if goals are effectively set and managed, desired results will follow. It is better to establish smaller and more obtainable targets in order to maintain an intense focus on desired outcomes and results. Once achieved, new goals and objectives can be established and implemented.

STRATEGIES, TIPS & TECHNIQUES TO APPLY

Goal setting does not require detailed or technical skills in order to accomplish specific desired results. A simple model can be used for professional planning. It includes three steps:

Know What Is to Be Accomplished

The key to successful goal setting is to be as clear and concise as possible in establishing what exactly is to be achieved. Goal setting is not a place to be vague. Goals are the focus of any planning process. They should be specific, measurable, realistic and attainable. As they tend to create multiple added frustrations, unrealistic goals only result in hindering effectiveness.

Often when sales managers set goals, they fail to consider the results once they are obtained. An additional pitfall is establishing goals that are more superficial in nature. Effective goals should have real meaning and purpose and need to create a positive impact once they are accomplished. This implies that as sales managers set personal or professional goals, they should plan ways to stretch their abilities to attain them.

Know What It Will Take to Achieve the Goal

Sales managers need to examine what steps are needed and what specifically must be accomplished in order to attain the goals they establish. Goals are designed to give sales managers a focus, direction and the impetus for making certain results a reality. Unto themselves they are merely "destinations." Sales managers need to plan the routes to arrive at these desired destinations. Individual checkpoints along the way are defined through the specific objectives required to achieve each individual goal.

Sales managers should define and establish a series of small and obtainable steps that directly lead to the achievement of their individual goals. They should be revisited often to determine if any additional activities, methods or skills are required to attain specific desired outcomes.

Set Deadlines

Goals established without attaching realistic deadlines are meaningless. They provide sales managers with an excuse to procrastinate. Deadlines create the pressure sales managers need to keep them focused and moving forward toward the accomplishment of positive results. Many overly ambitious sales managers tend to set unrealistic goals for themselves that fail to provide adequate time to effectively achieve them. They also fail to account for uncontrollable events that may suddenly impact their goals or delay their accomplishment.

As sales managers follow this simple goal setting model, they should consider dividing their goals into sub-goals. It is easier to follow through each sub-goal one step at a time until each ultimate goal is achieved. This also reduces the stress and anxiety that larger goals may place on them. Sales managers must continually remind themselves that the purpose of goal setting is to build upon individual successes in order to produce increased results. Goal setting is also intended to provide forward movement for their salespeople and companies.

Before the End of the Day...

Before the close of every business day, sales managers should do two things:

1. *Write down three objectives for the following day.*

Goals are achieved when sales managers are able to move themselves forward on a regular basis. Three objectives a day will help them progress on an ongoing basis. Any more than three tends to bog sales managers down.

Setting objectives at the end of the day provides sales managers direction, helps keep them focused, and provides a quick start for each new day. It allows them to focus on what needs to be done in a sequential time frame and reference. Minds and thoughts become set into effective work modes and are focused on what needs to be accomplished before actually beginning particular tasks and assignments. If sales managers choose to wait until each morning to begin establishing their agendas and defining their individual activities, they will need to jumpstart themselves to get back into a smooth flowing work mode and mindset. Most will have forgotten the thrust and direction of the previous day, which is needed to carry on each new day's tasks and assignments.

2. *Write down one objective for each of the next day's activities.*

Sales managers have full schedules. However, most phone calls, evaluations and activities in general are made without specific objectives in mind.

Sales managers should set specific obtainable objectives that keep them moving forward. All individual objectives should be defined from an action-oriented standpoint. The purpose behind them is to accomplish step-by-step movement that works to position sales managers closer to the accomplishment of individually defined goals.

Defined objectives may include ones allowing them to advance their companies' goals, while helping them to consistently monitor the pulse of what their people are doing. Some objectives might be focused on getting specific answers to pressing questions, or feedback on pending issues. Others might be focused on gaining commitments for product tests or necessary coaching or mentoring in order to improve individual salespeople's skills. Whatever the reason, daily objectives should move sales managers forward a step or two at a time toward the accomplishment of their established goals.

POINTS TO PONDER – SOMETHING TO THINK ABOUT

1. Do you feel you are disciplined in planning your work? Do you consistently plan daily activities and required responsibilities, or is your planning more inconsistent and erratic?
2. Do you see any benefits in carefully planning your daily departmental activities and time? Explain.

TRAINING ACTIVITY – APPLICATION & ACTION PLAN

Establish goals using the three-step planning model detailed above. Once this has been accomplished, perform the following exercise for the next thirty days:

- Write down three objectives ahead of time for each daily agenda.
- Write down one objective for each of your next day's activities.

It will take discipline to get through the first month, after which you will begin to set goals and objectives more routinely and without the need to push or force yourself. The process will eventually become automatic, increasing your productivity and allowing you to manage and organize your time more efficiently. Getting into this habit will also aid in reducing accompanied goal attainment stress and frustration.

3

Maximizing Your Time Means Setting Priorities

One of the biggest complaints most sales managers have is the lack of time to perform their tasks and responsibilities during a typical business day. Most can recognize the obvious ways time is wasted on unproductive tasks. Yet, how many are impervious to time wasters that sap this valuable resource, such as numerous meetings, unproductive time management, or working on assignments at wrong or inappropriate times?

Sales managers able to recognize how their time is spent can take the first step in effectively managing it, while eliminating most hidden time wasters.

IMPLICATIONS — WHAT THIS MEANS TO YOU

Sales managers wasting the least amount of time have the most to gain. Good organization—including long- and short-range planning as well as setting priorities—is absolutely necessary for eliminating time-wasting tasks. It is critical to think about tomorrow, next week and into the future, setting objectives and anticipating needs before they occur.

But planning and preparation are not enough. Sales managers must have the personal determination and discipline to work their plans and resist activities that do not advance their goals.

This is important because the first priority of sales managers is to achieve their goals in order to maximize results and performance. During the normal course of business, it is all too easy to become absorbed in unproductive activities that tend to take the focus away from their primary priorities.

STRATEGIES, TIPS & TECHNIQUES TO APPLY

Effective personal management requires sales managers to constantly evaluate their workloads, which includes establishing a list of priorities for each day. To be most effective, when workloads are light they should use the available time to follow up and organize their assignments, responsibilities, activities and thoughts in order to avoid cutting into more crucial management time.

Sales managers can use the following proven techniques to carefully manage their time:

Goals and Objectives

Sales managers must be able to establish clear and concise goals and objectives, and review them frequently. They must continually question whether certain activities will move them closer to their major goals and objectives. If they do not, they need to eliminate them. Where possible, sales managers should organize their time in 15-minute blocks. One block of time per hour or for a day's activities is inadequate for proper time management.

Meetings

Countless meetings often serve only to bog sales managers down. Many are compelled to arrive at the office early and stay late just to handle their phone messages, correspondence and emails. Sales managers must determine whether their presence is essential before agreeing to attend particular meetings, with those that are unnecessary avoided. Where possible, delegated salespeople should be assigned to attend on their behalf. When attendance at a meeting is required, it should be scheduled to run only long enough to meet specific preset objectives.

Delegation

Sales managers must learn to delegate nonessential tasks that do not directly advance them toward the attainment of major goals and objectives. Where and when possible, they should utilize their salespeople's talents, skills and abilities for increasing their unit's overall effectiveness.

Prime Time

Sales managers need to use their valuable time managing their salespeople. Sales managers hurt themselves when they do other people's work for them or waste time on unnecessary activities.

Use of Time Management Aids

Sales managers must use technology to increase their overall effectiveness. This includes using the phone, email, faxes, call management systems and other tools to aid in making the most productive use of their time. Where possible, sales managers should send their dictations and notes to assistants to be entered into their companies' existing contact systems. Saving an hour a day by doing this adds a half a day per week of management time.

POINTS TO PONDER — SOMETHING TO THINK ABOUT

1. How often do you analyze your time by using and reviewing a daily activity log?
2. Do you analyze your activities to assure that you are maximizing the use of your time?

TRAINING ACTIVITY – APPLICATION & ACTION PLAN

1. Nightly or weekly, whenever you plan your activities, ask this simple question of every item on your calendar or agenda: "Does this activity move me forward to the successful accomplishment of my major goals?"
2. Score each item on your calendar. Remove, delegate or cancel those activities that do not move you forward.

4

Meet the Onslaught of Paper Head-On

Most sales managers are forced to fight daily waves of paperwork. It seems that today, salespeople as well as top management officials all "want it in writing." Memos are written, copied, mailed and filed. Letters fly out of the office as fast as they are prepared. Invoices, inventory requests, reports of every nature and production schedules require reams of paperwork. This paperwork continues to pile up higher and higher, which makes everyone involved more and more frustrated.

IMPLICATIONS — WHAT THIS MEANS TO YOU

Oftentimes inordinate amounts of paper are generated simply out of habit. The problem is, sales managers often have too much information to sort through in too little time. Pitney Bowes conducted a survey that indicated that most sales managers typically receive over 200 phone calls, emails, letters and faxes every business day. With most requiring some kind of written response, it is little wonder why sales managers feel overwhelmed in their job-related activities.

In slower economic cycles, levels of paperwork tend to escalate as sales managers fearing layoffs or downsizing begin to create paper trails to document their work. This is often an attempt to substantiate their "worth" if and when decisions surface regarding possibly eliminating their jobs.

STRATEGIES, TIPS & TECHNIQUES TO APPLY

For the sake of maintaining efficiency and productivity, it is essential for sales managers to create a quality paperwork management system. This starts with them personally generating as little paperwork as possible. With the following additional simple changes, sales managers should begin to feel far less bogged down and see their performance improve.

Focus on the Desired Results

Sales managers have the primary responsibility of producing increased results. When dealing with paperwork, a piece of paper should be handled once, and once only. If upon scanning the paper it becomes apparent the information is not immediately applicable to their specific targeted goals or the results they are working toward, it should either be delegated to the proper subordinate or disposed of. Making this a daily habit will save valuable time.

Ask Whether Necessary

The next time sales managers are tempted to write a memo or a letter, they should ask themselves, "What is the worst thing that will happen if I do not send this?" If the answer is "essentially nothing," they should stop. Unnecessary documentation is a leading cause of paper overwork and overload. It has been proven over and over again that most information currently being documented has already been documented elsewhere.

Sales managers should furthermore avoid devoting time to sending emails or writing memos when a quick phone call or meeting will take less time and often have more impact. Instant responses save time, energy and stress. Additionally, using these tools allows sales managers to immediately paraphrase, clarify and question other individuals to make certain there are no gaps or errors in understanding and communication.

Conduct Unnecessary-Paper Screening

Using the following techniques, duplicates of reports, assignment requests, procedural summaries, mailed pieces and other paperwork can be eliminated to help keep the clutter down to a manageable amount.

Sales managers should:

- Prepare a priority list of the paperwork they feel is absolutely necessary to handle.
- Not pick up a piece of paper without moving it out of the way—permanently. If sales managers are unsure if a piece of paper needs to be kept, more often than not it is safe to discard.
- Sort out the paperwork that needs immediate attention and prioritize the selected pieces in order of their importance.
- Create one stack and begin working on it.
- Remove their name from various mailing lists, reading lists and promotional materials that are deemed unimportant and/or unnecessary.

Resist the Urge to Copy

Designed to be an efficient method for handling office paperwork, copying machines have unfortunately also become enormous paper generators. Copying tends to hinder rather than increase effectiveness, as it is most likely that what will be copied will never need to be referred to again. When tempted to make an extra copy for safekeeping, sales managers should bear in mind this only creates extra baggage to be toted around until the appropriate place to file it (which in fact often requires an altogether new file) can be found.

Practice the Art of Dictation

While driving or sitting with a few moments to spare, sales managers can dictate short letters on a tape recorder. It is easier to organize essential parts of important correspondence while ideas are fresh in your mind. This saves numerous attempts in printing and revising copies, while reducing the number of letters that require grammatical or spelling changes and thought alterations.

POINTS TO PONDER — SOMETHING TO THINK ABOUT

1. Do you personally feel overwhelmed by the levels of paperwork you are currently receiving and/or generating?
2. How efficient are you in managing the time and energy it takes to handle all of your paperwork?

TRAINING ACTIVITY — APPLICATION & ACTION PLAN

To help reduce paperwork frustration and overloads:

- Eliminate copying reports, plans and other paperwork to help keep the clutter down to manageable quantities.
- Prepare a priority list of the paperwork you feel is absolutely necessary to handle.
- Sort out the paperwork that needs your immediate attention.
- Prioritize the selected pieces in order of their importance.
- Create one stack and begin working on it.
- Remove your name from various mailing lists, reading lists and promotional materials that you find unimportant.

5

Effective Delegation Can Save Your Sanity

Many sales managers have an aversion to delegating assignments and responsibilities. They generally can find a variety of reasons why they choose to get things done on their own. Perhaps it is because they tend to cling to the philosophy that hard work is considered a virtue, where they feel they are the only ones that can get things done expediently and effectively in the exact way they want without added time and frustration. Some sales managers may have a fear of delegating because in previous situations the wrong individuals were selected to accomplish certain tasks or projects, which produced more problems than the actual assignments were worth. Other sales managers may have a tendency to feel impossible workloads often openly suggest and demonstrate their superiority in the workplace, which are attitudes that become hard to break.

IMPLICATIONS – WHAT THIS MEANS TO YOU

Many sales managers are under ever-increasing pressure to perform and attain results. Economic and competitive conditions have a tendency to increase workloads, frustrations and the need for enhanced time management practices. Sales managers are often forced to become involved in more strategy sessions and meetings, where their feedback is continually being sought. This only works to drain their desire and energy to perform to the best of their abilities.

The most effective way for sales managers to free themselves from increasing pressures and burdens is to either eliminate them altogether or delegate certain responsibilities to competent salespeople. Knowing how to delegate successfully is crucial, since the process is able to expand their ability to increase personal efficiency and overall productivity.

STRATEGIES, TIPS & TECHNIQUES TO APPLY

Failure to delegate can oftentimes result in sacrificing one's indispensability. A review of effective techniques may offer some usable ideas when sales managers are faced with the decision or necessity to delegate.

First, sales managers should make certain to identify the right person to delegate to. It is important not to confuse the best candidate for the job as one who necessarily comes at a higher price or appears to have superior experience. If individuals do not personally fit the specific characteristics required for particular delegated tasks and responsibilities, the outcomes will not be in the sales manager's favor.

Sales managers should check carefully to make sure that the individuals delegated to have the proper training to complete their assignments in the time allowed, with little need for direction and intervention. The right match of skills and motivation is essential, with what will be accepted as satisfactory performance defined ahead of time.

It is essential to accurately and clearly define the nature and scope of delegated tasks and responsibilities. If time is not given to initially explain particular expectations, or if delegated individuals do not ask the appropriate specific questions regarding their assignments, odds are the jobs or tasks will take longer and yield poor results, which will most likely produce a backlash.

Oftentimes it is far more effective to use varying degrees of delegation. It is important to remember that sales managers can delegate small responsibilities as well as more complex, detailed projects and assignments. For smaller delegated tasks, it is easy to use the "Will you look into this?" approach or the "Please recommend a course of action" approach. Getting feedback on something is all you may need at certain times.

A "take action" approach can be reserved for larger delegated responsibilities. With more complex assignments or projects, it is essential to make sure there is a collective understanding by all parties involved as to the particular type of approach to be used, as well as to fully define how much responsibility is involved and the expected timeline of completion dates.

Once particular tasks or responsibilities have been delegated, sales managers should not forget to give credit to the individuals who completed the work successfully. Sincere recognition will enhance a reputation for fairness, trust and effectiveness. Recognizing and rewarding productive, positive behaviors increases the odds for successfully reapplying them in future situations. Delegated workers will generally perform harder than ever to meet the standards set in order to sustain the positive personal belief sales managers have in them.

Sales managers should avoid assigning meaningless tasks to their people. This openly suggests a pretense of delegation. When assigning given tasks, they should be worthy of the delegated salesperson's ability, time and effort. Sales managers should let salespeople know how valuable their time, energy, and the efforts needed to complete their assignments are. They should offer the necessary support to allow the individuals to complete their jobs in the easiest and most effective manner possible.

Sales managers should take action against "reverse delegation." Once tasks are assigned, there should be no reason to have them "boomerang back." If this happens, sales managers can simply acknowledge the situation with, "I gave you this to do because I wanted to see how you would handle it." It should be followed with helping the particular individuals to identify strategies, methods and best practices for completing assignments in an efficient and timely fashion. This strengthens their decision making skills and reduces the time spent in dealing with their ongoing indecision or associated work-related problems.

Sales managers should always remember to assign tasks and responsibilities by requesting rather than ordering. This demonstrates a sense of inward respect and outward courtesy. As end results will still fall upon the sales managers' shoulders, they should make sure to follow up on responsibilities.

The final step in delegating is to check on the performance of the allocated work. When doing this, it is helpful for sales managers to refer to as many "who, what, where and when" questions as they can think of in order to gain proper and insightful feedback. The skillful use of proper and extensive questioning is the most crucial basis for having delegated projects completed successfully.

POINTS TO PONDER – SOMETHING TO THINK ABOUT

1. Do you perform tasks that could otherwise be easily delegated because you feel they will be done easier and faster?
2. What has been your overall experience in delegating tasks and responsibilities? Has the process been relatively successful? Were the resulting assignment outcomes favorable?

TRAINING ACTIVITY – APPLICATION & ACTION PLAN

Carefully examine your current calendar and "to do" list. Determine certain activities and tasks that can be delegated.

1. Review the capabilities of your salespeople.
2. Determine which activities can be effectively delegated to your salespeople according to their particular skills, levels of motivation and abilities.
3. Begin by selecting one task and one candidate.
4. Sit down with the candidate as you delegate the selected task, activity, project or assignment.
5. Develop a specific action plan to follow.
6. Together with the salesperson, agree to what needs to be done.
7. Detail the specific steps defining how it will be done.
8. Explain and discuss the reasons why.

9. Follow up with the delegated salesperson to determine if the agreed upon action plan is being followed closely.
10. Continually monitor the salesperson's progress.
11. When necessary, adapt, modify and correct the plan until the delegated task, assignment or project is completed.
12. Conduct a follow up meeting to review the salesperson's performance.

6

Make Your Next Meeting a Success

Departmental meetings can run the gamut from boring to exciting, ranging from sales managers rushing through agendas to dramatic multimedia displays. Most are somewhere in between. Meetings in any form are expensive and time-consuming. Sales managers cannot afford to approach meeting planning and presentations haphazardly.

IMPLICATIONS – WHAT THIS MEANS TO YOU

Organizational meetings are generally designed to cover a host of topics, such as imparting and sharing specific information, management directives or actual production or training delivery. At the very least, meetings need to become the catalyst for "stirring the pot," inducing sales managers to think of ways to motivate themselves, increase their overall performance and find new approaches, methods and ideas that may work more effectively. Good meetings tend to balance space, time, specific learning styles, information and entertainment.

This is important for sales managers to consider because effective meetings are designed to teach and inform—not entertain. Care should be taken to insure that information imparted becomes retained over greater periods of time. Otherwise, only the peripherals that are meant to enhance the meetings, such as dinners, entertainment and non business-related activities, will be remembered in the long-term.

STRATEGIES, TIPS & TECHNIQUES TO APPLY

There are several rules to follow when planning and presenting effective meetings which work to make them more successful. All meetings should include:

Objectives

All meetings should be designed with specific purposes and objectives in mind. These should be stated in one or two simple sentences.

Agendas

All meetings should be well-planned and have specific agendas attached that are distributed to all attendees at least one week in advance. Meetings should never ramble aimlessly without specific points or purposes behind them. A lack of focus or direction results in sales managers critically damaging their professional credibility as strong and effective leaders.

Expertise

Many sales managers do not possess a balance of overall wide-range expertise. They may be highly effective in specific areas but can easily fall short in others. Because of it, they should determine and analyze their professional strengths, in-depth knowledge, competencies and proficiencies, as well as their personal familiarity with all essential meeting-related topics. If there is a perceived weakness, they should seriously consider using outside sources to fill in the gaps to make particular meetings more meaningful and purposeful. If budgets do not exist for outsourcing, sales managers should consider using professionally prepared training programs to assist them in preparing and presenting quality programs.

Specifics, Not Generalities

It is important to avoid generalities. Sales managers need to maintain a focus on information that is specific, interesting and useful. They should keep meeting members' concentration levels in mind and avoid "information overload."

Sales managers should also make it a point to avoid lengthy speeches that accompany production number breakdowns or other topics that tend to require close, detailed addressing, identification and analyzing. Handouts are better for imparting certain types of detailed information. However, it is important to leave room for notes, questions, comments and/or actions underneath points of discussion, in the margins or at the end of individual sections.

Activities

Whenever possible, sales managers are advised to limit their meetings to no more than two hours. In order to break up boredom and maintain higher attention levels, they should include activities that keep attendees active and moving around. They should be specifically designed to entertain and teach. Longer sessions should be broken into smaller, applicable learning segments.

Learning Styles

Sales managers should use slides and videos to enhance their presentations. They need to understand and recognize that individuals learn differently: some by hearing, others by seeing, and still others through tactile hands-on experience. Sales managers need to balance their presentations by appealing to all the senses and diverse learning styles of their particular audience members.

Attitudes

Sales managers should make it a point to continually stress the positive. This is especially important during down periods as well as during times of high pressure. If meetings tend to include complaints about a lack of revenue, overall negative results or a loss of orders, they only end up demotivating attendees. Sales managers should continually focus on starting and ending their meetings on an upbeat, positive note.

Atmospheres

Within meetings, sales managers need to play up the "team" aspect. They should never reprimand or embarrass individuals. Meetings are not the time or place for finger-pointing. They are intended to gather positive feedback, impart information and generate effective solutions or ideas. It is important to remember that all negative behaviors must be avoided and not tolerated within specific meeting environments.

Environments

Sales managers should never underestimate the impact meeting environments have on being able to attain their overall objectives. Where particular meetings are held sends a subliminal message. A well-appointed facility indicates sales managers assign a high value to their salespeople's contributions. A low-budget venue demonstrates a lack of concern or respect for their people and their efforts.

As training and travel budgets shrink, sales managers need to find an acceptable middle ground for meeting facilities. As holding meetings at higher-dollar facilities may no longer be economically feasible, it is possible to step down a level or two without sacrificing the desired image sales managers wish to maintain.

Rehearsals

All presentations—especially those made for senior sales managers—should be well-prepared and rehearsed. Rehearsals allow sales managers to effectively time their presentations, polish their topics and actually hear the material as it is being presented. It also helps them to practice their tone, resonance, emphasis, gestures and movements. This is what separates run-of-the-mill meetings from superior, professional efforts.

Follow Up

Most training is forgotten within 30 days. Sales managers must make sure they offer follow-up training and coaching for ongoing reinforcement. This assures that training investments are protected and that specific meeting objectives are met.

Surveys

As a final step, sales managers should conduct follow-up surveys of all attendees in order to determine their honest reactions to individual meetings. This input should be used to improve and enhance future meetings.

> **POINTS TO PONDER – SOMETHING TO THINK ABOUT**
>
> 1. How do you plan and prepare for your meetings?
> 2. Have your past meetings been as effective as you wanted them to be? Why or why not?

TRAINING ACTIVITY – APPLICATION & ACTION PLAN

Review your general meeting strategies. How do you:

1. Determine meeting purposes, agendas and objectives?
2. Determine meeting frequency and feasibility?
3. Go about identifying and selecting appropriate facilities for your meetings?
4. Provide resource individuals who bring additional expertise into your meetings when needed?
5. Determine how these individuals are selected?
6. Involve salespeople in planning or presenting specific topics or material?

7

Does This Activity Move Me Forward?

While sales managers need to have an internal focus that advances them toward the overall accomplishment of their goals and objectives, many continually get bogged down with a myriad of meetings, phone calls and peripheral activities. Rather than actively advance them toward particular goals, their activities tend to be concentrated on dealing with daily crises and unexpected events. This results in a complete loss of focus and direction.

IMPLICATIONS — WHAT THIS MEANS TO YOU

Time is one element that can actively control sales managers' daily lives, when in essence, *they* should be controlling and regulating *it*. Time management is something that can easily spin out of control as the complexities of the job overtake fulfilling daily schedules, accomplishing tasks and completing necessary assignments on their active "to-do" lists. Because it happens incrementally, sales managers unwittingly become controlled by commitments and events, rather than effectively managing their time as the one resource indispensable to their success.

Over time, sales managers tend to commit or get obligated to a number of tasks and activities that incrementally sap their valuable time. This diminishes their personal effectiveness, which results in an overall loss of productivity. Most sales managers are not even aware that their effectiveness is steadily deteriorating.

STRATEGIES, TIPS & TECHNIQUES TO APPLY

All sales managers should have a system or method to effectively manage their time and activities. Whether on the back of an envelope or with a Palm Pilot, they need to have a system that organizes, schedules and plans their various daily activities. As everyone tends to have individual styles as to how they choose to stay organized, perform their work and complete their activities, the system selected should be one that is best suited to their work style. If sales managers are not comfortable with a specific planning system, they will not use it effectively—if at all. The reality is, no matter the individual preference, or what was spent on a particular planning and management system, it ultimately still remains a big "to-do" requiring proper management.

Most sales managers use various types of planning systems because they are keyed toward specific time and activity control and management. However, one thing these systems cannot do is prioritize daily activities. Few sales managers actually take the time to weigh or categorize the activities on their Day Timers or Day Runners.

Without the essential step of priority setting, any planning system is useless. Many sales managers appear busy and no doubt are, but waste much of their time on tasks and projects that do not advance them toward their primary goals. Consequently, many tend to accomplish things that have no real value or impact on their professional lives and careers.

One technique that is effective in maximizing time and efficiency includes a simple activity: every night or week, whenever sales managers plan their activities, they should ask this simple question regarding every item on their calendar or agenda, "Does this activity advance me forward to the successful accomplishment of my major goals?"

As they apply this question in regard to every item on their calendars, each item should be scored with a "yes" or "no." If the answer is negative, sales managers should immediately remove, delegate or cancel those particular activities. This simple technique identifies the specific pursuits that are wasting their time and effort.

It should be noted that many activities are "addictive" and difficult to break away from. However, being busy does not always equate to effectiveness. Sales managers must transform their daily activities into ones that have a direct impact on the accomplishment of particular goals that are able to produce positive professional end results.

POINTS TO PONDER — SOMETHING TO THINK ABOUT

1. What priorities and responsibilities generally control most of your daily activities?
2. Are current demands and expectations contributing to or detracting from your personal management effectiveness?

TRAINING ACTIVITY — APPLICATION & ACTION PLAN

1. For the next thirty days, whenever you plan your activities, ask whether each one advances you toward the attainment of your goals.
2. Score each item. If the answer to a particular activity is negative, immediately remove, delegate or cancel it. Do the same for all others that do not move you toward the accomplishment of your set objectives.

8

The Most Effective Use of Time

The most effective use of time comes from sales managers' abilities to establish and detail appropriate and concise objectives. Making things happen that might otherwise go unattained, objectives allow sales managers to focus on obtaining results.

Many sales managers waste time by setting and following objectives that are unclear, imprecise or too broad. Objectives are reliable measurement tools for monitoring progress and directional courses of action. Time is used unproductively when sales managers' objectives are incompatible with organizational purposes and direction. Taking charge and authority over time comes from establishing appropriate departmental objectives.

IMPLICATIONS – WHAT THIS MEANS TO YOU

Exerting a direct influence on attitudes and motivation, appropriate objectives direct sales managers' efforts toward achieving concrete goals. Appropriate and effective objectives act as factors of success and become sustained positive attitude builders. They generate a consistency of action—which feeds continuous ongoing success—and prevent sales managers and their teams from performing random activities and making ineffective decisions.

Detailed objectives keep sales managers on track and alert to potential interferences that can be addressed early before they create serious problems. This maintains workplace momentum and keeps productivity at peak levels. Additionally, effective objectives allow sales managers to concentrate on future opportunities and establish new goals as future needs occur.

Determining sound daily, weekly and monthly objectives and following them takes work and discipline on the part of the sales manager. In order to advance personal performance and departmental efficiency sales managers must continually revisit all short- and long-term objectives.

STRATEGIES, TIPS & TECHNIQUES TO APPLY

Managing by objectives carries a positive impact in terms of saving time and increasing results. Sales managers should establish prioritized objectives to save work and reduce redundancies and frustrations. Objectives should be detailed carefully to assure essential assignments are met on a continual basis in all major areas.

Techniques to help establish time-saving departmental objectives include:

Establish Compatible Objectives

Sales managers must make certain that all objectives reflect how their own particular departments interrelate with others. Determining interrelated objectives will prevent departments from becoming independent operating units focused on meeting their own particular time schedules, quality standards and procedures. Valuable time and energy can be wasted because of segmented functions and disjointed compatibility.

When departmental incompatibility exists, time and attention is not devoted to organizational problem solving. Sales managers spend excessive amounts of time dealing with immediate crises and resulting conflict or chaos. Major issues tend to go unresolved and need more time and energy to remedy at a later time. As the need to produce results becomes pressured and forced, departmental cooperation and unity of effort is hindered.

Lay a Solid Groundwork for Defining Departmental Objectives

Objectives need to address departmental functions and purposes within the organization. Before determining departmental objectives sales managers need to ask themselves, "Why does my department exist?" Next, sales managers need to ask, "What should this department accomplish from an organizational standpoint?" To answer these questions, sales managers must define departmental expectations, agendas, functions, methods and procedures. Sales managers must make certain that they contribute in a positive way to the effective use of human resources and profitability. To be effective and more time sensitive, objectives must detail all necessary activities that contribute to overall organizational goals, as well as specific departmental ones.

Define Areas of Responsibility

Sales managers need to detail areas of departmental responsibility and identify particular key areas both where unnecessary overlaps occur and where overlaps should occur and do not. Within the analysis process, sales managers must concentrate on identifying areas of activity that play a significant role in achieving results. Valuable amounts of time can be saved and transformed into bottom-line profit. Objectives must detail necessary lead time for obtaining such things as raw materials, essential components, additional equipment and human resources.

Define Specific Departmental Functions

Sales managers need to assess departmental functions that are necessary for attaining determined goals and results before formalizing objectives. While addressing specific functions that are necessary for accomplishing their individual departmental missions, they concentrate on planning, organizing, directing and controlling these functions. Departmental objectives should address how each particular function will be performed and why as well as major areas of performance accountability.

POINTS TO PONDER — SOMETHING TO THINK ABOUT

1. How much time do you feel is saved by planning out departmental objectives?
2. Do you scrutinize daily activities and observe how time is spent in relationship to your departmental objectives and mission?

TRAINING ACTIVITY — APPLICATION & ACTION PLAN

1. Take the time to review and analyze your departmental mission. On a sheet of paper list the following items:
    - Its overall function
    - Its overall purpose
    - What it should accomplish
    - Its organizational interrelationships
    - Its role within the organization
    - Its areas of major accountability and responsibility
    - Its contribution to organizational progress
2. Use this information to develop detailed objectives to better maximize personal as well as departmental time and productivity.

About the Author

Timothy F. Bednarz, Ph.D. is CEO of the American Management Development Group, Inc. For over 20 years he has researched, designed and authored hundreds of learning and development programs used by Fortune 1000 companies.

He is also the author of *Great! What Makes Leaders Great. What They Did, How They Did It and What You Can Learn from It* (2011).

Speaking Availability

Timothy F. Bednarz, Ph.D. is available for speaking engagements for your next meeting or association event. He can be contacted at 800-654-4935 or by e-mail at timothy.bednarz@majorium.com.

Bulk Sales

Bulk sales of this book or any other titles available from Majorium Business Press. Inquiries can be directed to sales@majorium.com, or by phone at 800-6654-4935.

Quick Order Form

Fax orders: 715-342-1118. Send this form.

Telephone orders: Call 800-654-4935 toll-free. Have your credit card ready.

Email orders: sales@majorium.com

Postal orders: Majorium Business Press, 2025 Main Street, Stevens Point, WI 54481, USA.

Please send the following books:

____

____

____

____

Please send more FREE information on:

❑Catalog ❑Speaking/Seminars ❑Mailing Lists ❑Consulting

Name: ____________________________________

Address: __________________________________

City: ____________________ State: ____ Zip: ________

Telephone: ________________________________

Email address: ______________________________

Sales tax: Please add 5.5% for products shipped to Wisconsin addresses.

Shipping by air:

United States: $4.00 for first book and $2.00 for each additional product.

International: $9.00 for first book; $5.00 for each additional product (estimate).

Made in the USA
Monee, IL
04 November 2026

67377557R00031